Life Cycles of Living Things

Mammal Life Cycle

Tracy Vonder Brink

Table of Contents

A Starfish Book

SEAHORSE PUBLISHING

Teaching Tips for Caregivers:

As a caregiver, you can help your child succeed in school by giving them a strong foundation in language and literacy skills and a desire to learn to read.

This book helps children grow by letting them practice reading skills.

Reading for pleasure and interest will help your child to develop reading skills and will give your child the opportunity to practice these skills in meaningful ways.

- Encourage your child to read on her own at home
- Encourage your child to practice reading aloud
- Encourage activities that require reading
- Establish a reading time
- Talk with your child
- Give your child writing materials

Teaching Tips for Teachers:

Research shows that one of the best ways for students to learn a new topic is to read about it.

Before Reading

- Read the "Words to Know" and discuss the meaning of each word.
- Read the back cover to see what the book is about.

During Reading

- When a student gets to a word that is unknown, ask them to look at the rest of the sentence to find clues to help with the meaning of the unknown word.
- Ask the student to write down any pages of the book that were confusing to them.

After Reading

- Discuss the main idea of the book.
- Ask students to give one detail that they learned in the book by showing a text dependent answer from the book.

Mammal Life Cycle

All living things are born.

They grow to be adults.

We call these changes a life cycle.

Mammals are animals with backbones.

They have fur or hair.

Mammals are **warm-blooded**.

Mammals have bigger brains than other groups of animals.

A mammal's life cycle begins with an **embryo**.

The embryo grows inside the mother mammal.

The mother gives birth.

The newborn mammal has the same **features** as an adult.

But it cannot yet live on its own.

Some mammals have one baby at a time. Others have many babies.

Mammals are the only animals that make milk for their young.

The mother's body makes milk.

The newborn **nurses** from the mother.

The young mammal drinks milk until it is old enough to eat other foods.

One or both parents must care for it.

The parents teach their young how to be adults.

The young mammal becomes a **juvenile**.

One or both parents continue to care for it.

It grows larger and learns to do what adult mammals do.

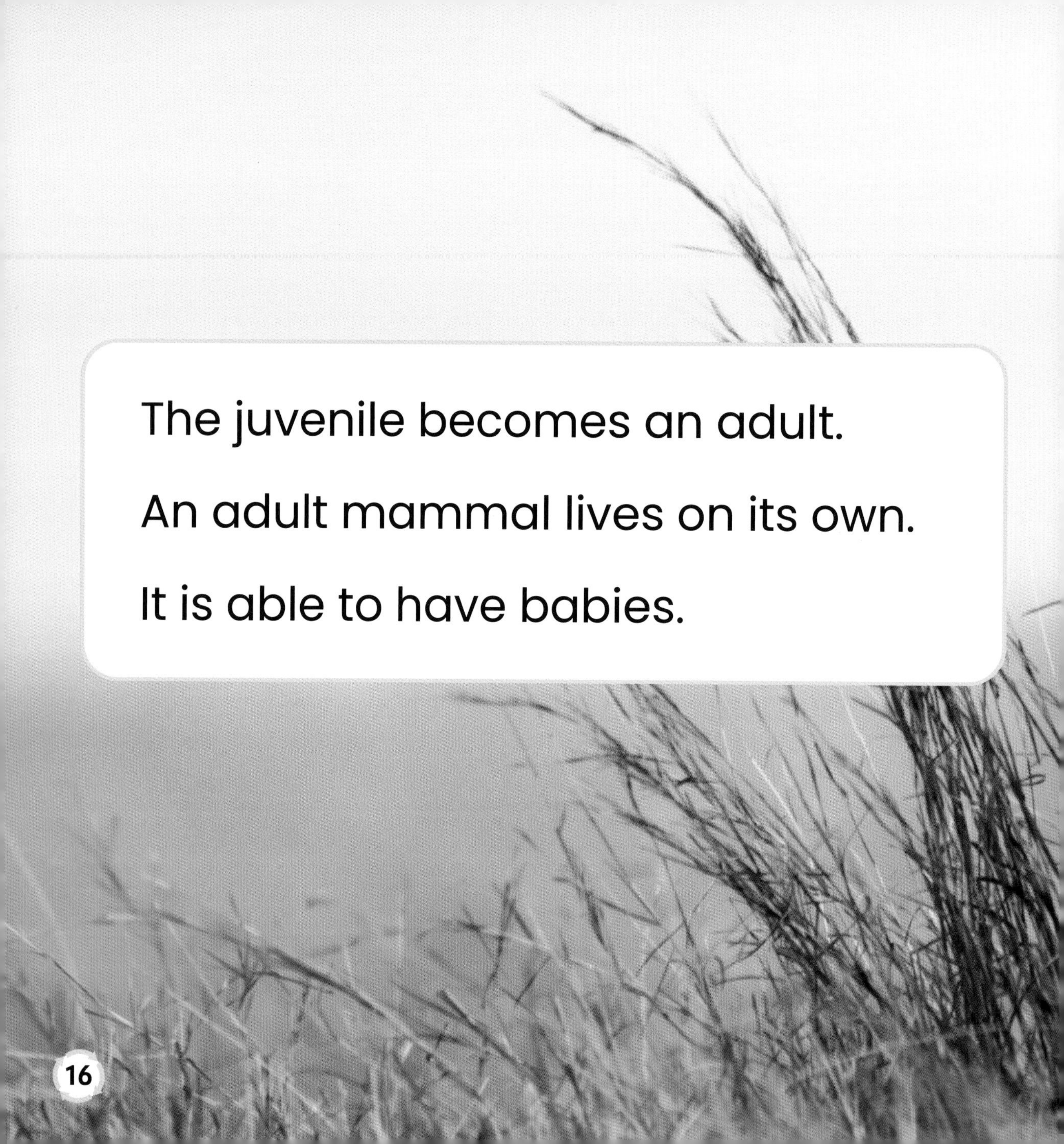

The juvenile becomes an adult.

An adult mammal lives on its own.

It is able to have babies.

Adult mammals look for mates.

Some keep the same mate for life.

The female becomes **pregnant**.

The life cycle begins again.

Words to Know

embryo (EM-bree-oh): a living creature in the earliest stage of development, before it is hatched or born

features (FEE-churz): parts, qualities, or characteristics; the features of an animal's body include its legs, tail, eyes, etc.

juvenile (JOO-vuh-nile): a young living creature that has not yet reached its adult form

nurses (NUR-sis): takes milk from a mother mammal

pregnant (PREG-nuhnt): having a baby developing inside a female's body

warm-blooded (worm BLUHD-id): able to make body heat; having a warm body temperature that does not change even if the surrounding temperature is very hot or very cold

Index

Comprehension Questions

1. A mammal grows
   a. underwater.
   b. inside the mother mammal.
   c. inside a hard-shelled egg.
2. Baby mammals
   a. are cared for by their parents.
   b. live on their own.
   c. live in a group.
3. Juvenile mammals
   a. learn to do what adult mammals do.
   b. live on their own.
   c. hunt with a group of other juveniles.
4. **True or false:** Mammals have hair or fur.
5. **True or false:** A juvenile mammal can have babies.

Answers

1. b 2. a 3. a 4. True 5. False

About the Author

Tracy Vonder Brink loves true stories and facts. She has written more than twenty books for kids and is a contributing editor for three children's science magazines. Tracy lives in Cincinnati, Ohio, with her husband, two daughters, and two rescue dogs.

Written by: Tracy Vonder Brink
Design by: Bobbie Houser
Editor: Kim Thompson

Photographs:
t = Top, b = Bottom, c = Center, l = Left, r = Right

Shutterstock: Art Babych: cover tl; Kenton D. Gomez: cover tr; Jim Cumming: cover b; Abeselom Zerit: p. 3 l; Ocean Eloy: p. 3 c; Eric Gevaert: p. 3 r; David Rasmus: pp. 4-5; John Michael Vosloo: p. 7; finepic: p. 9; James Copeland: p. 10; Tony Campbell: p. 13; Alan Jeffery: p. 14; Maggy Meyer: pp. 16-17; Richard Seeley: pp. 18-19; KBA: p. 21

Library of Congress PCN Data
Mammal Life Cycle / Tracy Vonder Brink
Life Cycles of Living Things
ISBN 978-1-63897-455-0 (hard cover)
ISBN 978-1-63897-570-0 (paperback)
ISBN 978-1-63897-685-1 (EPUB)
ISBN 978-1-63897-800-8 (eBook)
Library of Congress Control Number: 2021953368

Printed in the United States of America.

Seahorse Publishing Company
www.seahorsepub.com

Published in the United States
Seahorse Publishing
PO Box 771325
Coral Springs, FL 33077

SEAHORSE PUBLISHING